FURNITURE MAKING
ADVANCED PROJECTS IN WOODWORK

By
Ira S. Griffith, A.B.

The Manual Arts Press
Peoria, Illinois
1912

Introduction by Gary Roberts
2011

The Toolemera Press

From Our Personal Library To Yours

www.toolemera.com

Furniture Making: Advanced Projects In Woodwork
by Ira S. Griffith
1912

No part of this book may be reproduced, stored in an electronic retrieval system, or transmitted in any form or by an means, electronic, mechanical, photocopy, photographic or otherwise without the written permission of the publisher.

Excerpts of one page or less for the purposes of review and comment are permissible.

Copyright © 2011 The Toolemera Press
All rights reserved.

International Standard Book Number
ISBN: 978-0-9831500-1-5
(Trade Paperback)

Published by
The Toolemera Press
Dedham, Massachusetts
U.S.A. 02026

http://toolemera.com

Manufactured in the United States of America

Introduction
by Gary Roberts

"The Purpose of all education is the better preparation of the student to meet his environment, present and probable future, as judged by society."
Ira S. Griffith: Manual Training Magazine. 1916; Vol. 17, p. 413

Furniture Making: Advanced Projects In Woodwork

One of a series of texts authored by Ira Griffith for use in the Manual Arts classroom /shop, *Advanced Projects In Woodwork* features the furniture and accessories of the Arts & Crafts period. Beginning with projects focused on basic hand skills and progressing to those that require greater thought and planning in execution, *Advanced Projects In Woodwork* provides five introductory exercises and forty-six measured drawings of Arts & Crafts furnishings.

Manual Arts and Arts & Crafts

Between 1910 and 1925, the Arts & Crafts movement in North America(more often known today as Craftsman style) was a predominant design aesthetic. At the same time, the influence of the Manual Arts movement on educational theory and practice was peaking. Manual Arts, the predecessor to Vocational Education, emphasized the importance of craft in the intellectual, social and physical development of students of both genders.

Often deceptively simple in appearance, but complex in the visual and practical interactions of the various design elements, Arts & Crafts style furnishings represented a departure from the often excessive ornamentation of the Gothic, Eastlake, Victorian and Arte Nouveau periods. Manual Arts educators applied the design and process elements of the Arts & Crafts ethos to the requirements of curriculum development: the item created should be doable by students possessed of increasing skill levels as well as being an object which could be put to use in every day life, thereby enhancing the relationships between craft, intellect, and society.

Ira Samuel Griffith : 1874-1924

Born in Kansas, Ira Griffith earned his A.B. degree from Eureka College, Illinois, in 1896. His primary influence was Charles Bennett, the major figure in the development of the Manual Arts movement in North America.

Griffith's career as an educator spanned 22 years, beginning as an Instructor in Mathematics, progressing to Instructor in Manual Arts and then to Chair of various university Departments of Industrial Education.

A widely published theorist as well as an advocate of the importance of the practical application of theory to classwork, Griffith authored a series of influential books which remain relevant today to the educational process, whether formal or avocational.

Toolemera Press Reprints

The Toolemera Press reprints classic books and ephemera on early tools, trades and industries. We will only reprint items held in our personal library. We will never use a source document from any online document depository. The Toolemera Press manages every aspect of the publishing process. All imaging is accomplished either in-house or by contract with respected document imaging services. We use Print-On-Demand to keep pricing affordable.

http://toolemera.com

FURNITURE MAKING
ADVANCED PROJECTS IN WOODWORK

By Ira S. Griffith, A. B.

Late Professor of Industrial Education, University of Wisconsin
Author of *Woodwork for Beginners, Essentials of Woodworking, Carpentry, Woodwork for Secondary Schools, Correlated Courses in Woodwork and Mechanical Drawing, Projects for Beginning Woodwork and Mechanical Drawing, Teaching the Manual and Industrial Arts.*

THE MANUAL ARTS PRESS
PEORIA, ILLINOIS

COPYRIGHT, 1912
IRA S. GRIFFITH
113P71

Printed in the United States of America

PREFACE

Furniture Making Advanced Projects in Woodwork is a collection of projects designed to meet the needs of classes in high school woodworking. These projects presuppose familiarity with woodworking processes, tools, and the two simple joints required in the making of projects contained in the author's *Projects in Beginning Woodwork and Mechanical Drawing*.

The drawings are complete only as to their general dimensions. The working out of details, such as the sizes of mortises and tenons and their locations, is left for the pupil in his work in drawing and design.

It is expected that the projects will afford suitable basic material for classes in woodworking design. It remains for the instructor to point out the manner in which this material may be used. For illustration, many beginning students are slow in appreciation of possible modifications in structure or decoration. Circular tops may be used instead of square or octagonal, and vice versa. Modification of the manner of filling side spaces with slats offers variety in initiative. Vertical posts may be made tapering and vice versa. Rails and stretchers may be variously employed. There is almost always a choice in the matter of joints,—keyed or thru or blind tenon. Fig. 1 is suggestive as to possible modifications of a type.

In addition to the possible structural modifications, the plates suggest variation in the matter of decorative ornament such as pierced and carved forms and simple inlay. Such ornament will, of course, be kept subordinate to the structural design.

The upholstering of stool tops and seats for chairs provides another problem in variation.

Little, if any, use is made of dowels as substitutes for the mortise-and-tenon. While it is true that modern commercial practice makes much use of dowels in this way, the author feels that such practice is too often contrary to the principles of good construction. Its genesis lies in economy of material rather than in any superiority as a fastening device.

In the designing of these projects the author has had in mind at all times the thought that most of the students using them would have access only to a band-saw or jig-saw and a miter-box in addition to the regular hand tool equipment. For this reason such projects as hall clocks, mission beds, etc., have been excluded. The exceptional student will find projects of sufficient size to tax his ability and muscle. Easier projects and

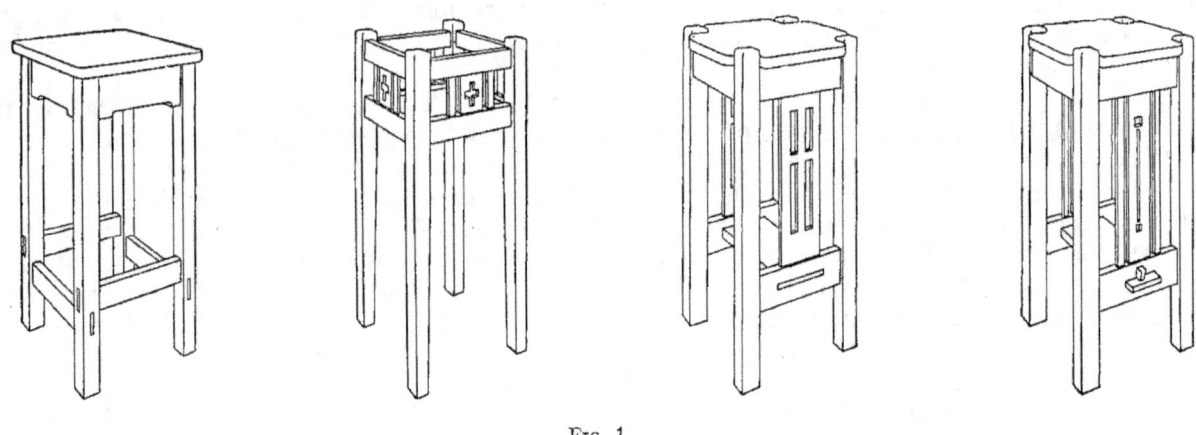

Fig. 1.

lighter projects have been provided for the weaker members of the class while the use of slats or their omission will provide additional variation in time of execution.

The use of stock ordered S-4-S (surfaced on four sides) has not been anticipated. The use of stock S-2-S and moldings such as are carried in stock by lumber yards is presupposed. If a working principle for the use of stock partly prepared were asked for it would be: Any material that is carried as stock and which does not have to be ordered especially worked for the project a boy elects or designs may be made use of legitimately. Such a principle would permit the use of stock S-2-S, moldings of stock pattern, hardware such as hinges and locks without any suggestion of deception. It would exclude table legs and tops, etc., especially prepared at a mill, and offers a rational dividing line between two extremes, neither of which is desirable.

Of course, these projects may be used in the teaching of the use of woodworking machinery.

No definite notes as to methods of procedure are given in this book for the student is supposed to have acquired, thru experience with the projects in the elementary book, enough insight to enable him to proceed on his own accord. Definite instruction in making the new joints, in wood-finishing, etc., will be found in *Essentials of Woodworking*, or *Woodwork for Secondary Schools*, companion books by the same author.

While these projects are especially arranged for use with the courses outlined and discussed in *Correlated Courses in Woodwork and Mechanical Drawing*, by the author, there is nothing in the form of the plates themselves to prevent their being used with any course in woodwork.

July, 1912

IRA S. GRIFFITH.

The inking of the drawings and the making of the perspectives in this book is the work of Mr. George Gordon Kellar.

LIST OF PLATES.

GROUP IX. — JOINERY.

1. Exercises — Keyed tenon, Blind Mortise-and-Tenon.
2. Exercises — Miter Joint, Glue Joint.
3. Exercises — Modeling, Hammer Handles.
4. Necktie Rack.
5. Footstool.
6. Book-rack.
7. Upholstered Stool.
8. Leg Rest.
9. Cricket.
10. Wall Shelves.
11. Stool (square).
12. Taboret (octagonal top).
13. Taboret (round top).
14. Small Table.
15. Taboret (square top).
16. Piano Bench.
17. Piano Bench.
18. Book stand.
19. Umbrella Stand.
20. Umbrella Stand.
21. Jardiniere Stand.
22. Magazine Stand.
23. Roman Seat.
24. Light Stand.
25. Stool (square).
26. Book Trough.
27. Screen.
28. Tea Table.
29. Hall Rack.
30. Wall China Rack.
31. Side Chair.
32. Arm Chair.
33. Morris Chair.
34. Electric Reading Lamp.
35. Pedestal.
36. Occasional Rocker.
37. Mission Chair.
38. Drop Leaf Table.

GROUP X. — CABINET WORK.

39. Exercises — Mortise-and-Tenon Joint, Rabbeted Joint, Grooved Joint.
40. Exercises — Thru Multiple Dovetail, Half-blind Dovetail.
41. Waste Paper Box.
42. Wall Cabinet.
43. Telephone Table.
44. Sewing Cabinet.
45. Writing Table.
46. Chafing-dish Stand.
47. Cabinet.
48. Library Table.
49. Writing-desk.
50. Dressing Table.
51. Linen Chest.

PRICE LIST FOR YEAR 19——, 19——

LUMBER — Quality, 1st, clear, and kiln-dried.

Kind of Wood	Per 1000 feet when surfaced on two sides							
Thickness in the Rough	⅜″	½″	⅝″	¾″	1″	1¼″	1½″	2″
Yellow Poplar								
White Pine								
¼ Sawed White Oak								
Mahogany								
¼ Sawed Red Sycamore								
Black Walnut								
Plain Sawed Red Oak								

HARDWARE —
    For prices on hardware consult Hardware Catalog provided for you.
    Figure retail price, that is, figure screws at price per dozen, not price per gross.

WOODFINISH —
    Per square foot of surface covered.

LABOR —
    Per hour.

(Form for high school use)

BILL OF MATERIAL

NAME_____   DATE BEGUN_____

CLASS_____   DATE FINISHED_____

ARTICLE_____   EXTRA HOURS_____

Pieces	Size	Description	Price	Feet	Cost	
2	½ x 3¼ x 12½	Walnut Slats S-2-S to ⅜ in.				
1	1 x 8¼ x 14½	" Stretcher " ⅞ in.				
6	1 x 3¼ x 12½	" Rails " "	.10	4.4	.39	
1	1 x 14¼ x 14½	" Top " "				
4	1½ x 1½ x 24½	" Posts " 1¼ in.	.11	2	.22	.66
8	2 inch No. 10	Flat Head Brt. Screws	.00½		.04	
4	1½ inch No. 10	" " " "	.00¼		.01	.05
	13 sq. feet	Wood Finish	.01			.13
		MATERIAL COST....				.84
	30 hrs.	Labor	.15		4	.50

TOTAL COST $5.34

INSTRUCTIONS FOR MAKING BILL OF MATERIAL.

Under "pieces" put the number of parts that are alike.

Under "size" put the various dimensions of pieces. In finding the sizes of the various pieces of lumber, examine the working drawings for finished dimensions, making due additions for tenons, then add $\frac{1}{4}''$ to the width and $\frac{1}{2}''$ to the length to allow for cutting out and squaring up. Tho you are to make use of stock mill-planed to thickness, you are to specify the thickness from which this mill-planed stock is got. Allow at least $\frac{1}{8}''$ for mill-planing.

Remember that length always means along the grain.

Fractions of an inch in width and length are not considered. Neither are fractions of a cent in the final results. If the fraction is $\frac{1}{2}$ or over, take the next higher whole number. If it is less than $\frac{1}{2}$, drop it. Fractions of an inch in thickness that are over $1''$ and fractions of a cent in the price per foot are to be figured as they are.

Lumber is measured by the superficial foot which is $1'' \times 12'' \times 12''$. Boards that are less than $1''$ thick are sold by surface measure. In other words, boards less than $1''$ thick are figured for quantity as $1''$ thick.

Standard sawed thicknesses are $1''$, $1\frac{1}{4}''$, $1\frac{1}{2}''$, $2''$, $2\frac{1}{2}''$, $3''$, $3\frac{1}{2}''$, $4''$. Thicknesses less than $1''$ necessitate resawing these sizes. In some communities the price per square foot for re-sawed stock varies for each difference of $\frac{1}{4}''$ in thickness.

In figuring, multiply the length by the width by the thickness, by the number of pieces. If any piece is less than $1''$ thick figure it as $1''$. Combine all results that are the same in price per foot. Reduce to square feet by dividing by 144. Reduce decimally and do not carry the result beyond tenths place. Dispose of any fractional part beyond tenths as directed above.

The price list gives the price of lumber per 1,000 feet. The price per foot is readily obtainable.

In figuring finish for these cabinet pieces, double the number of feet of stock as given by the stock bill to get the number of feet of finish. This is only an approximate method but is sufficiently accurate for such pieces as are to be made in first year high school, as specifed in Group IX of this book.

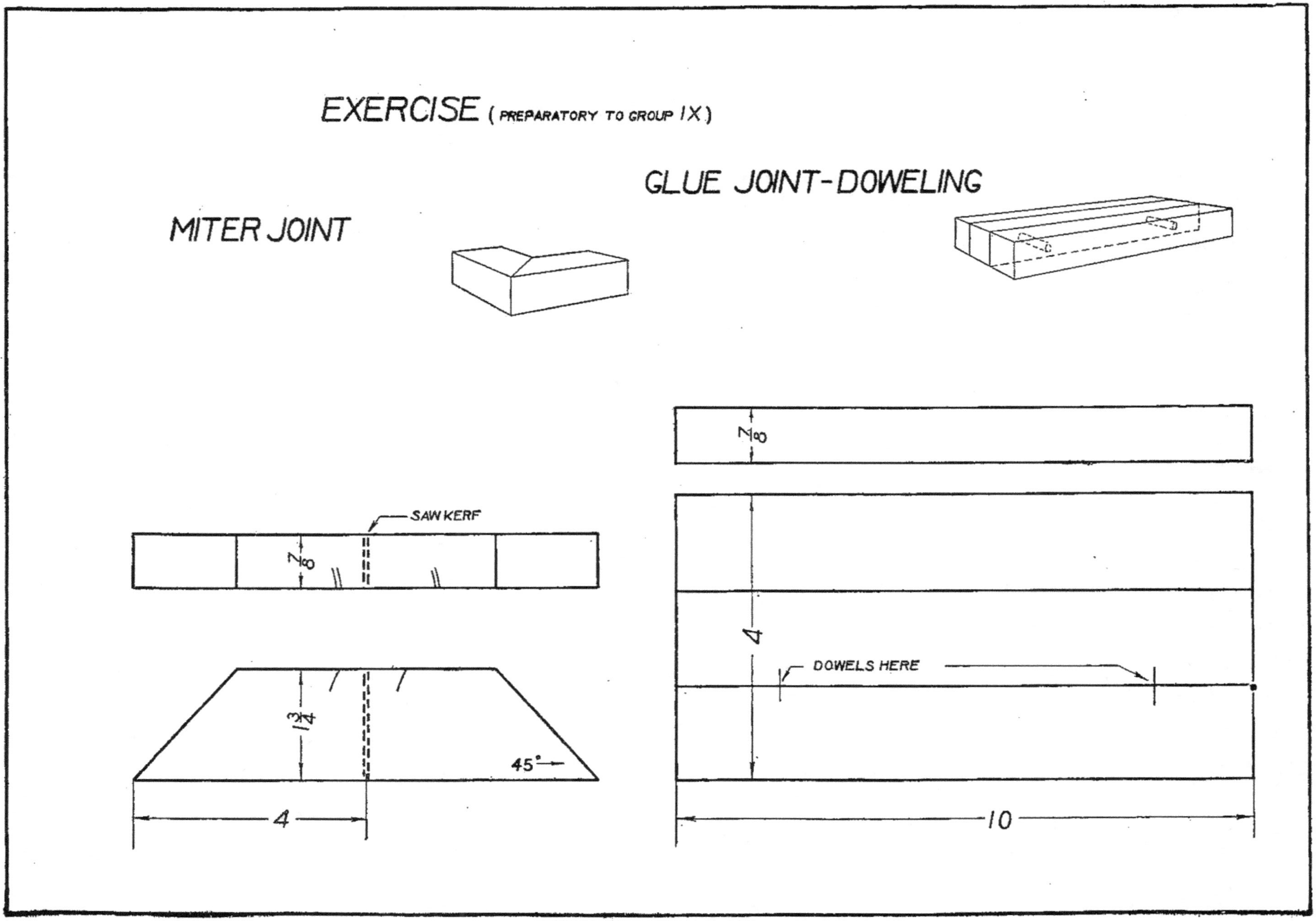

EXERCISE (PREPARATORY TO GROUP IX)
MITER JOINT
GLUE JOINT-DOWELING
SAW KERF
7/8
1 3/4
45°
4
7/8
4
DOWELS HERE
10

PLATE 2

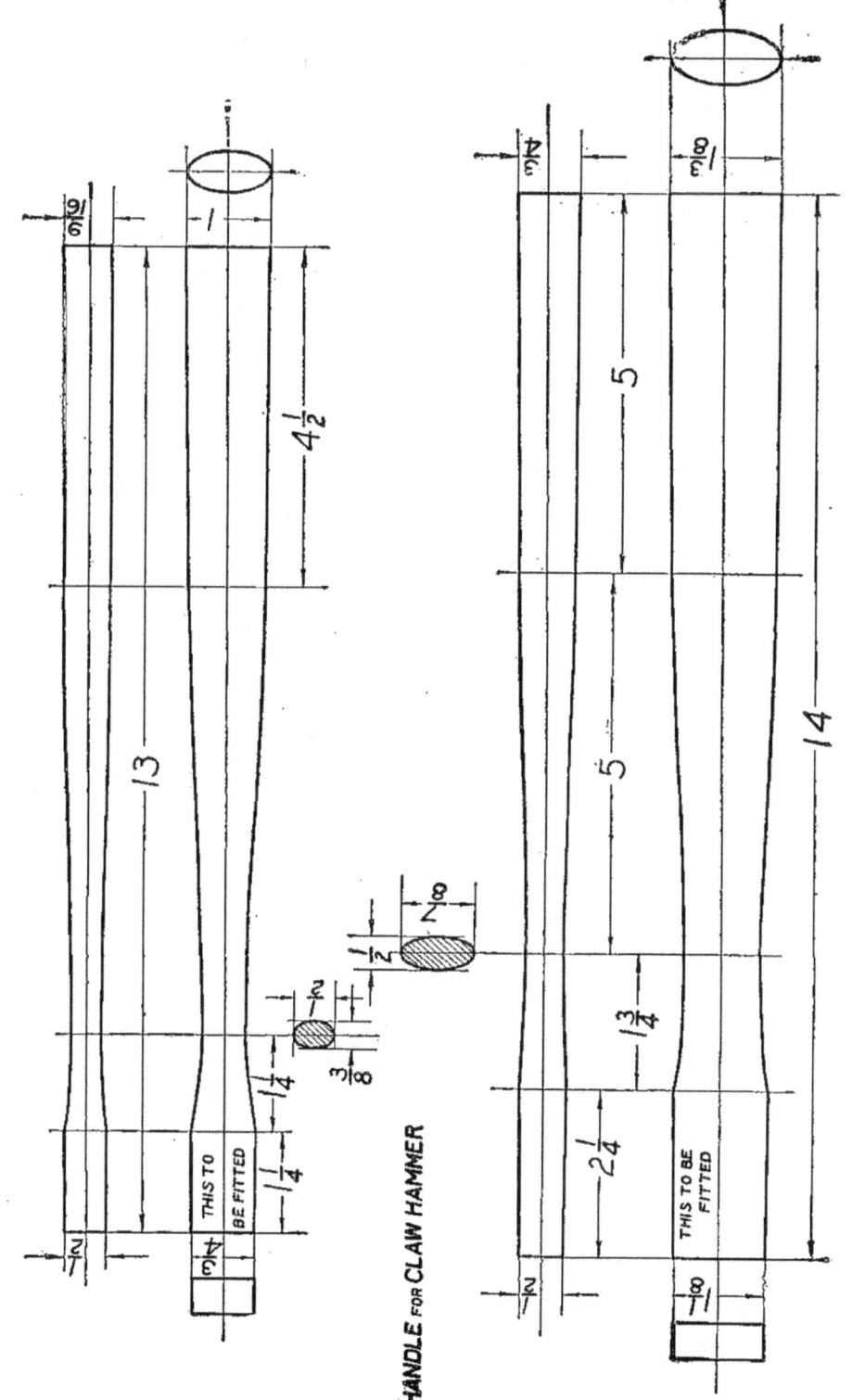

PLATE 3

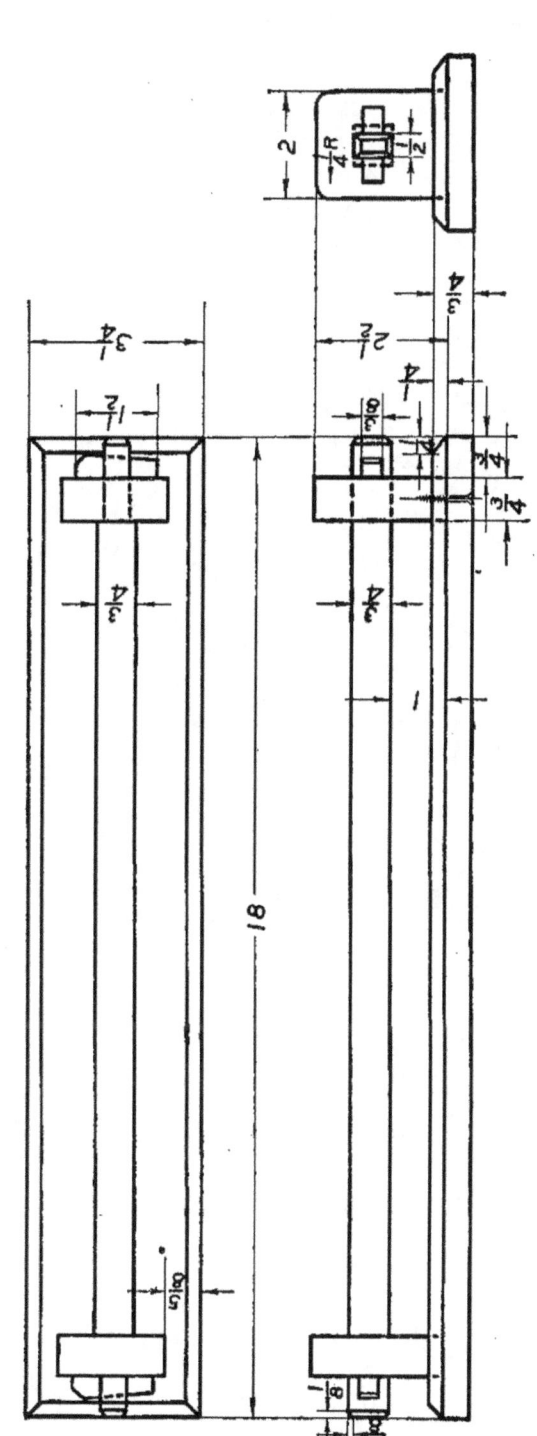

NECKTIE RACK

PLATE 4

FOOT STOOL

PLATE 5

BOOK RACK

PLATE 6

UPHOLSTERED STOOL

PLATE 7

LEG REST

PLATE 8

CRICKET

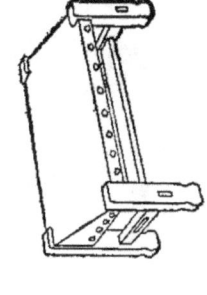
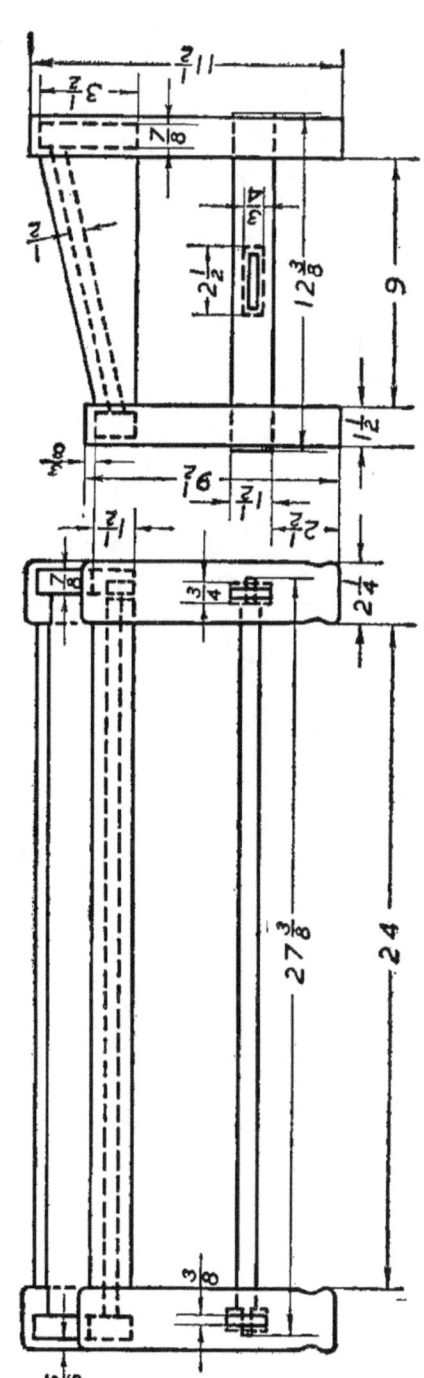

PLATE 9

WALL SHELVES

PLATE 10

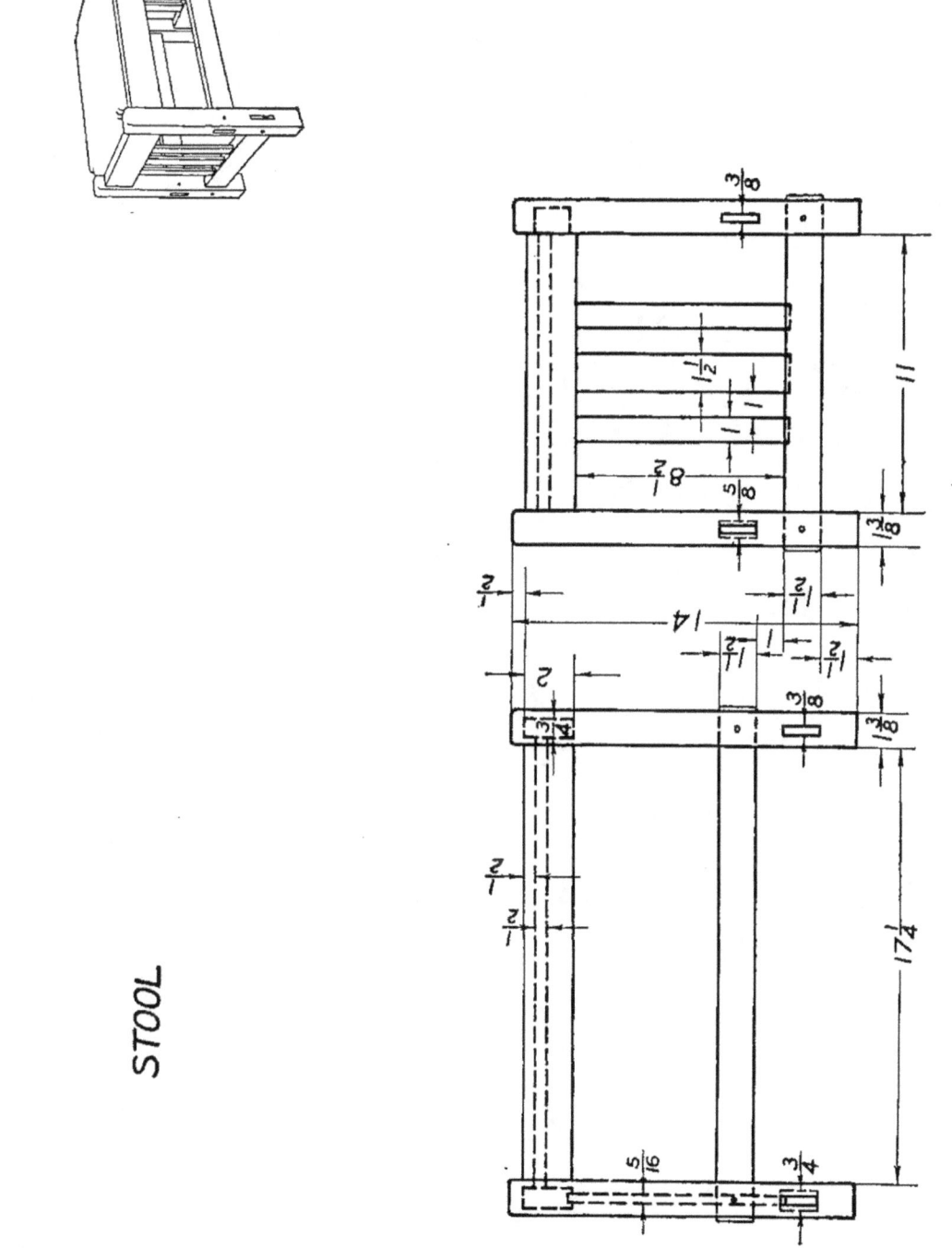

STOOL

PLATE 11

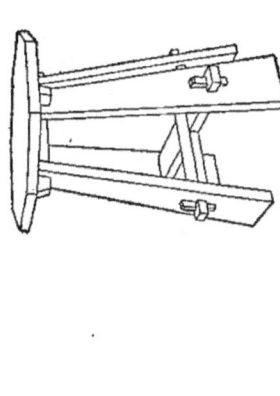

TABORET

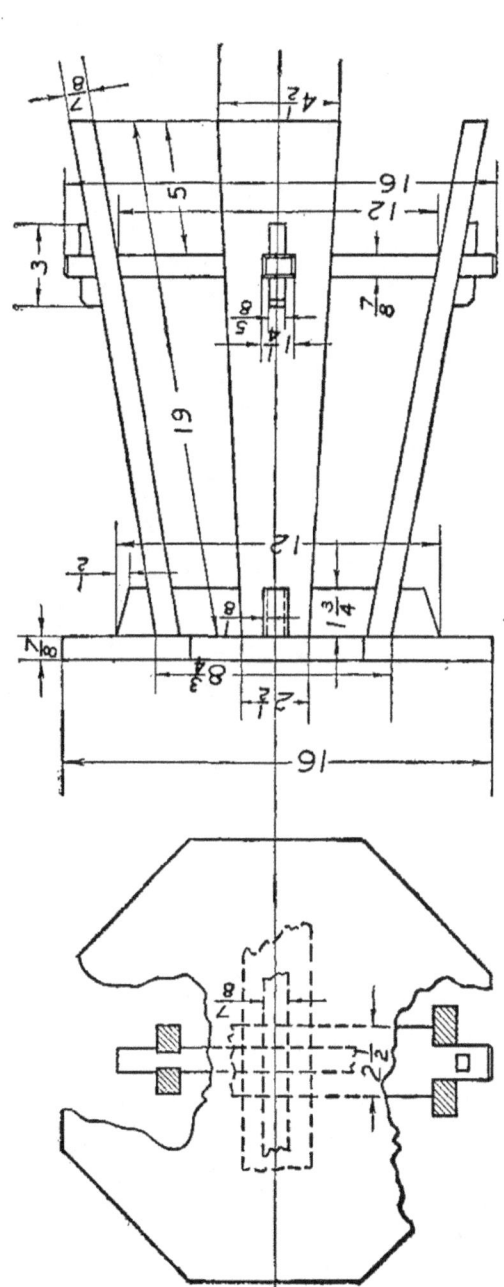

PLATE 12

TABORET

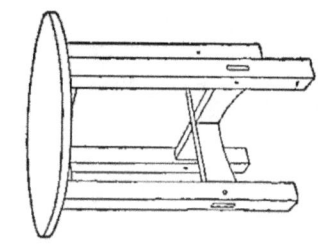
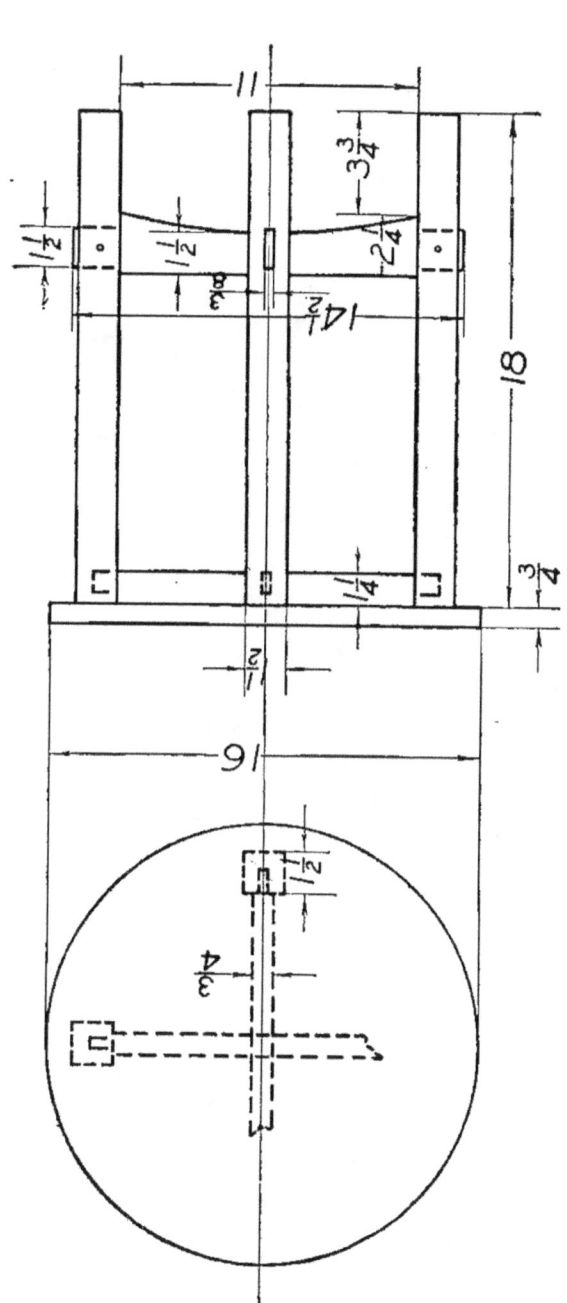

PLATE 13

SMALL TABLE

PLATE 14.

TABORET

PLATE 15

PIANO BENCH

PLATE 16

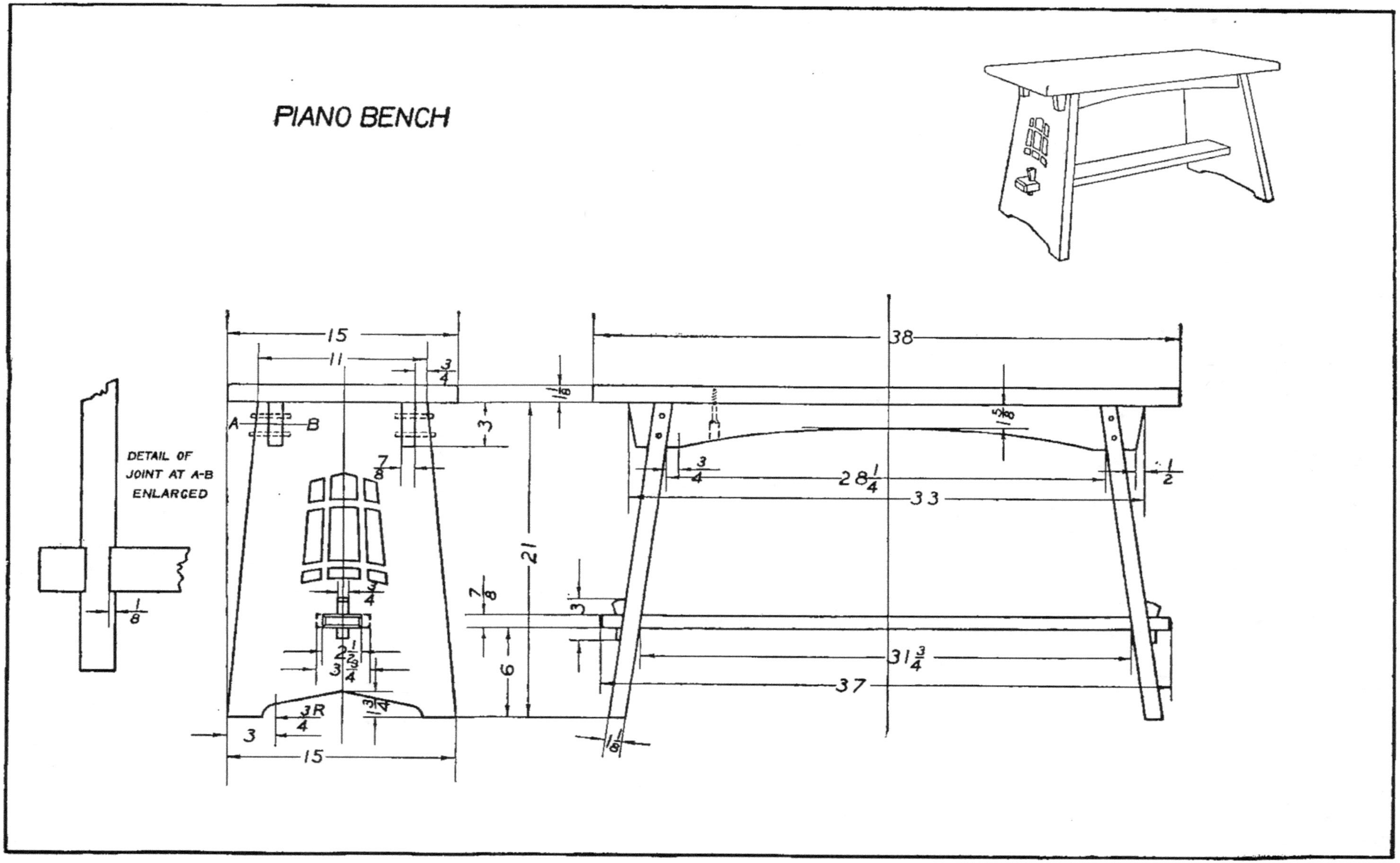
PIANO BENCH
DETAIL OF
JOINT AT A-B
ENLARGED
A
B
15
11
38
21
33
37
3

PLATE 17

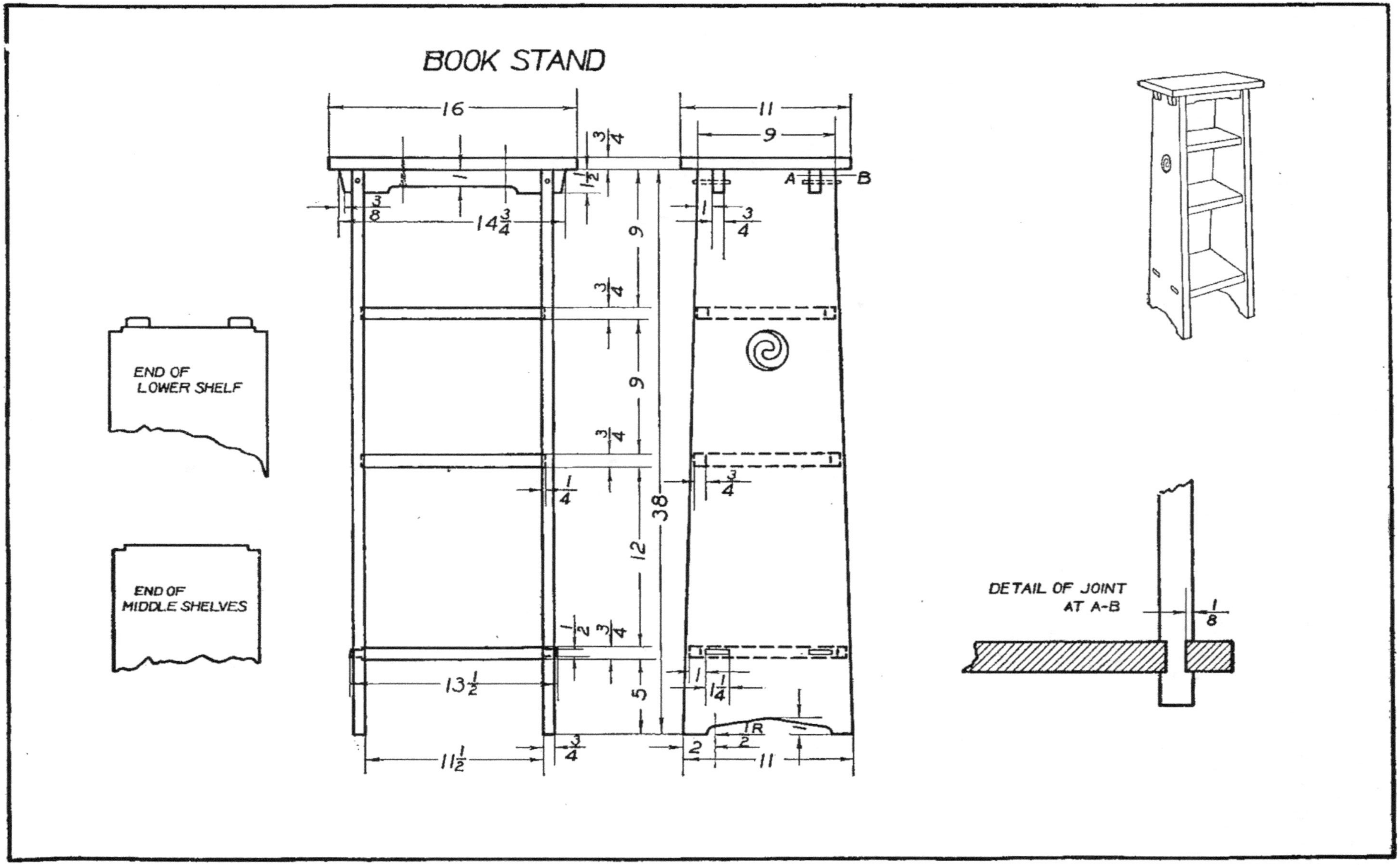

BOOK STAND

DETAIL OF JOINT AT A-B

END OF LOWER SHELF

END OF MIDDLE SHELVES

PLATE 18

UMBRELLA STAND

PLATE 19

UMBRELLA STAND

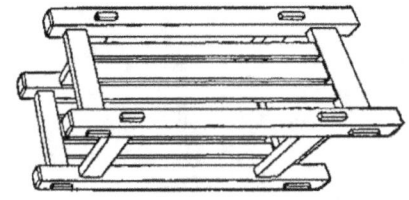

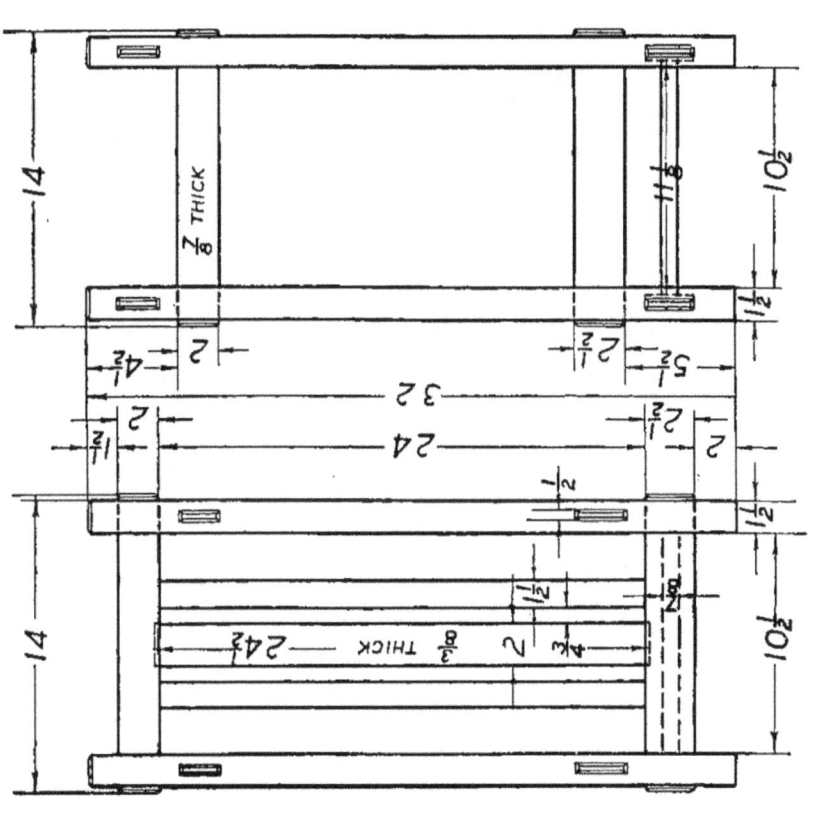

PLATE 20

JARDINIERE STAND

PLATE 21

MAGAZINE STAND

PLATE 22

ROMAN SEAT

PLATE 23

LIGHT STAND

PLATE 24

STOOL

PLATE 25

BOOK TROUGH

PLATE 26

SCREEN

PLATE 27

TEA TABLE

PLATE 28

HALL RACK

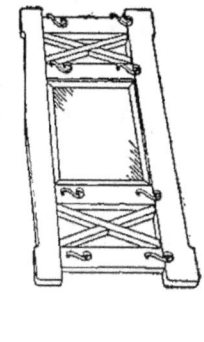
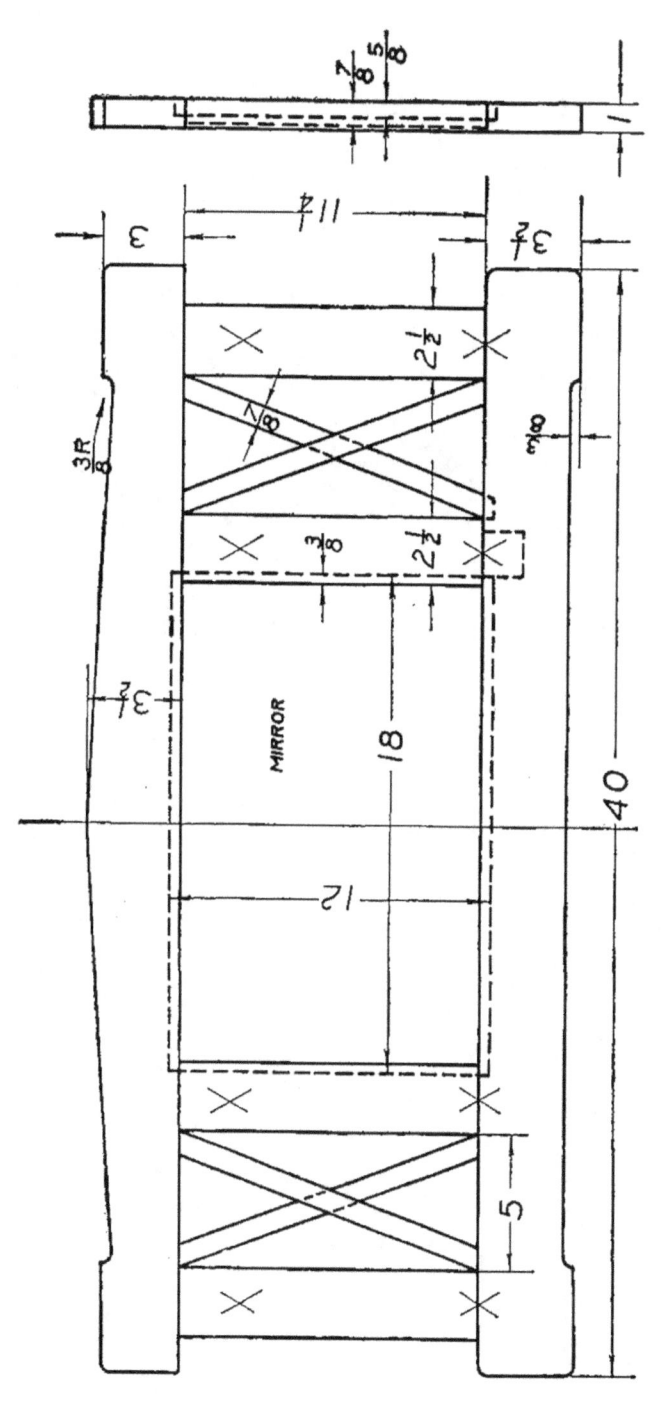

PLATE 29

WALL CHINA RACK
DETAIL OF A-B
A
B
2
2
3
40
$40\frac{1}{2}$
36
$23\frac{3}{4}$
$\frac{3}{4}$ SQUARE
$\frac{3}{8}$ SQUARE

Plate 30

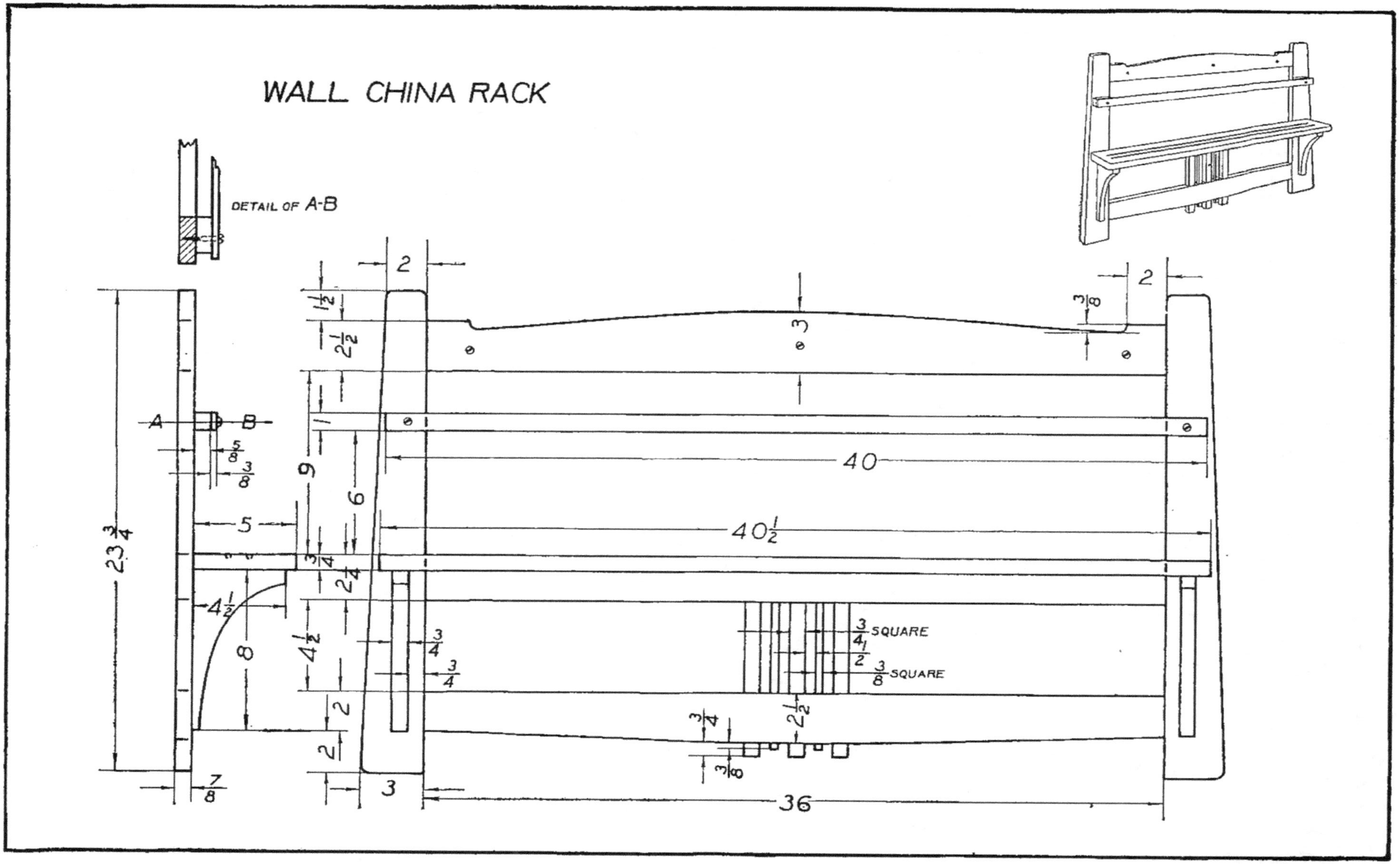

SIDE CHAIR

PLATE 31

ARM CHAIR

PLATE 32

MORRIS CHAIR

PLATE 33

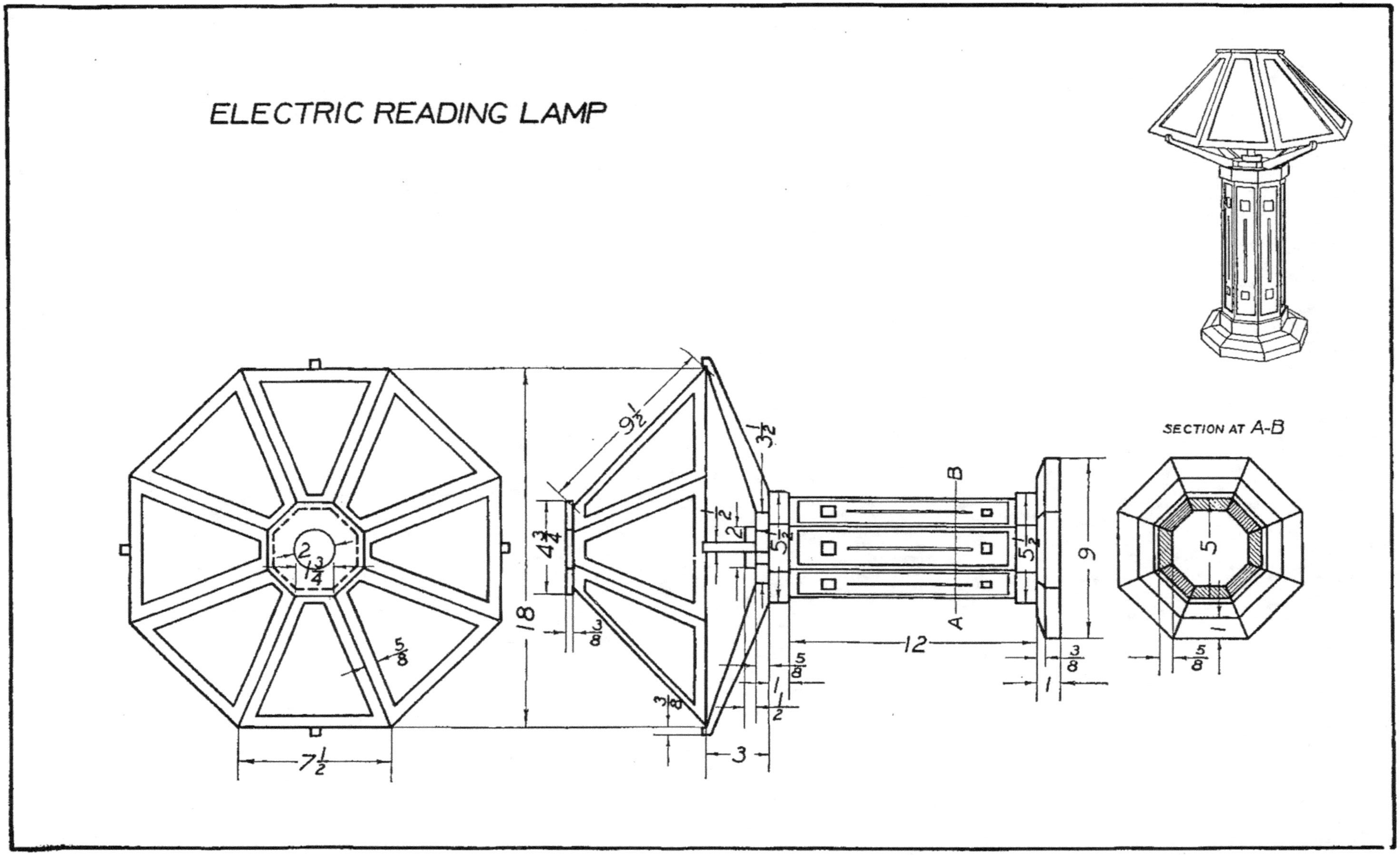
ELECTRIC READING LAMP
SECTION AT A-B
A
B
18
12
9
5
3
7½
9½
4¾
5½
3½
2
1¾
⅝
⅜
1
½

Plate 34

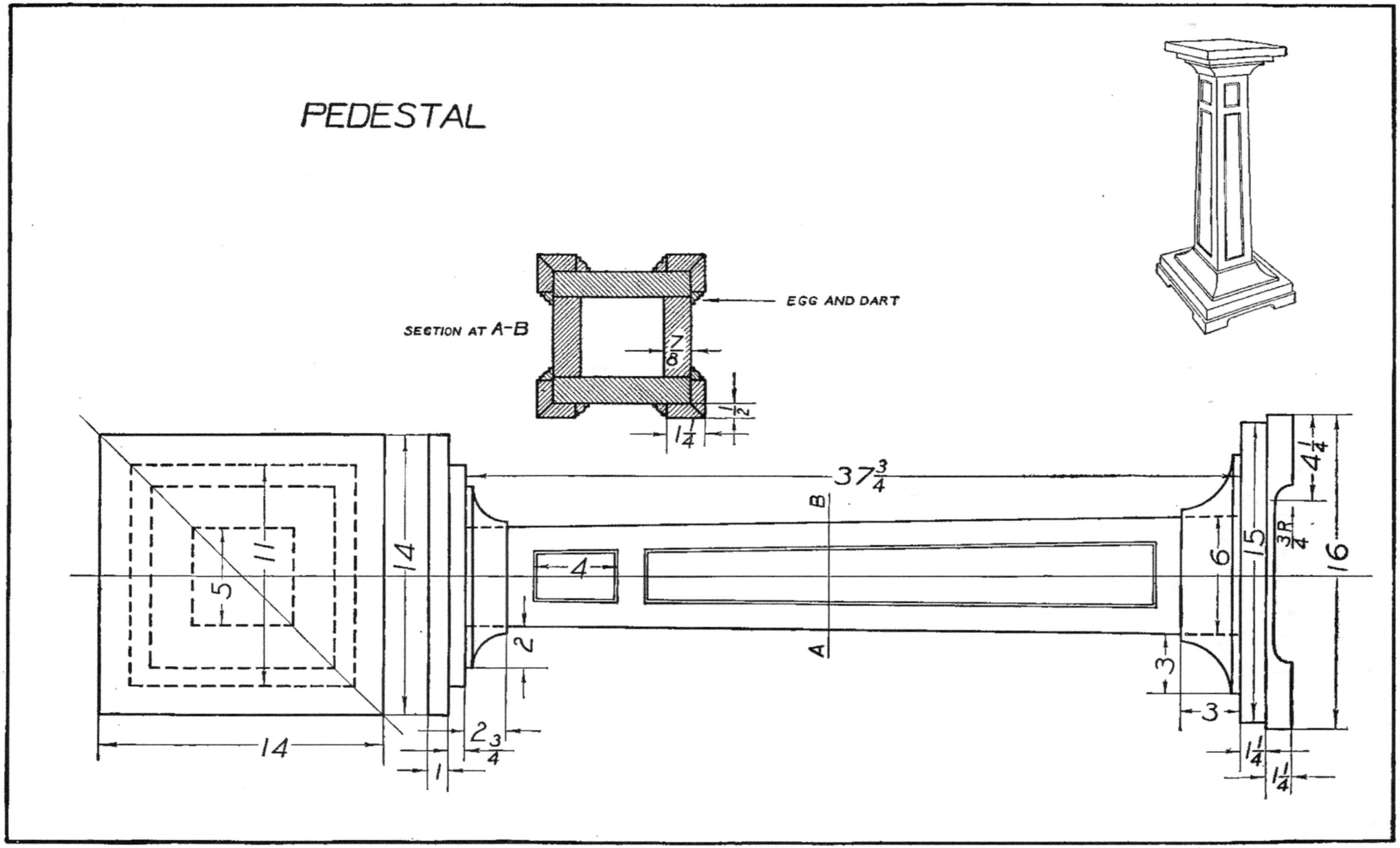
PEDESTAL
SECTION AT A-B
EGG AND DART
$37\frac{3}{4}$
16
15
14
14
11
6
5
4
3
3
2
1
$2\frac{3}{4}$
$1\frac{1}{4}$
$4\frac{1}{4}$
$\frac{3}{4}$R
$\frac{7}{8}$
$\frac{1}{2}$
A
B

Plate 35

OCCASIONAL ROCKER

PLATE 36

MISSION CHAIR

PLATE 37.

DROP LEAF TABLE

PLATE 38

EXERCISE – PREPARATORY TO GROUP X

MORTISE AND TENON–RABBETED

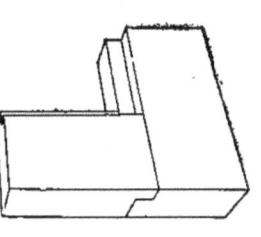

HAUNCHED MORTISE AND TENON–GROOVED

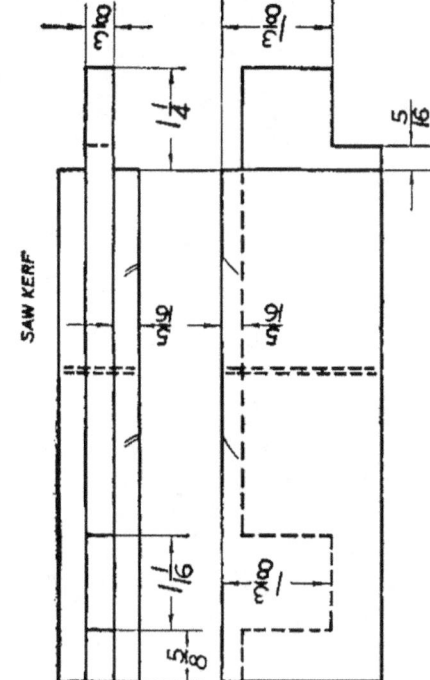

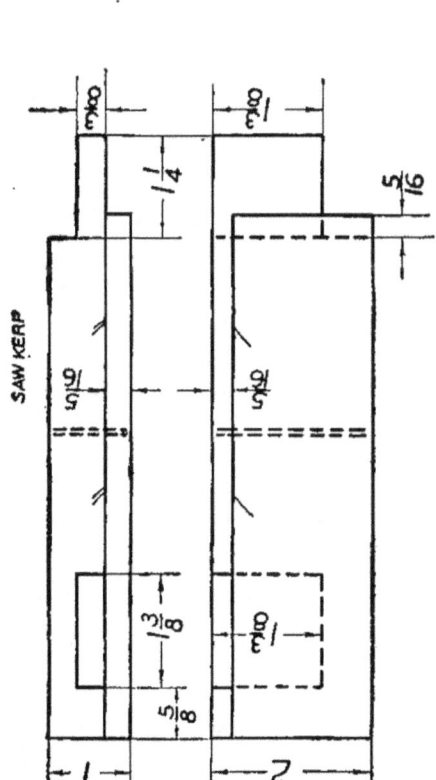

PLATE 39

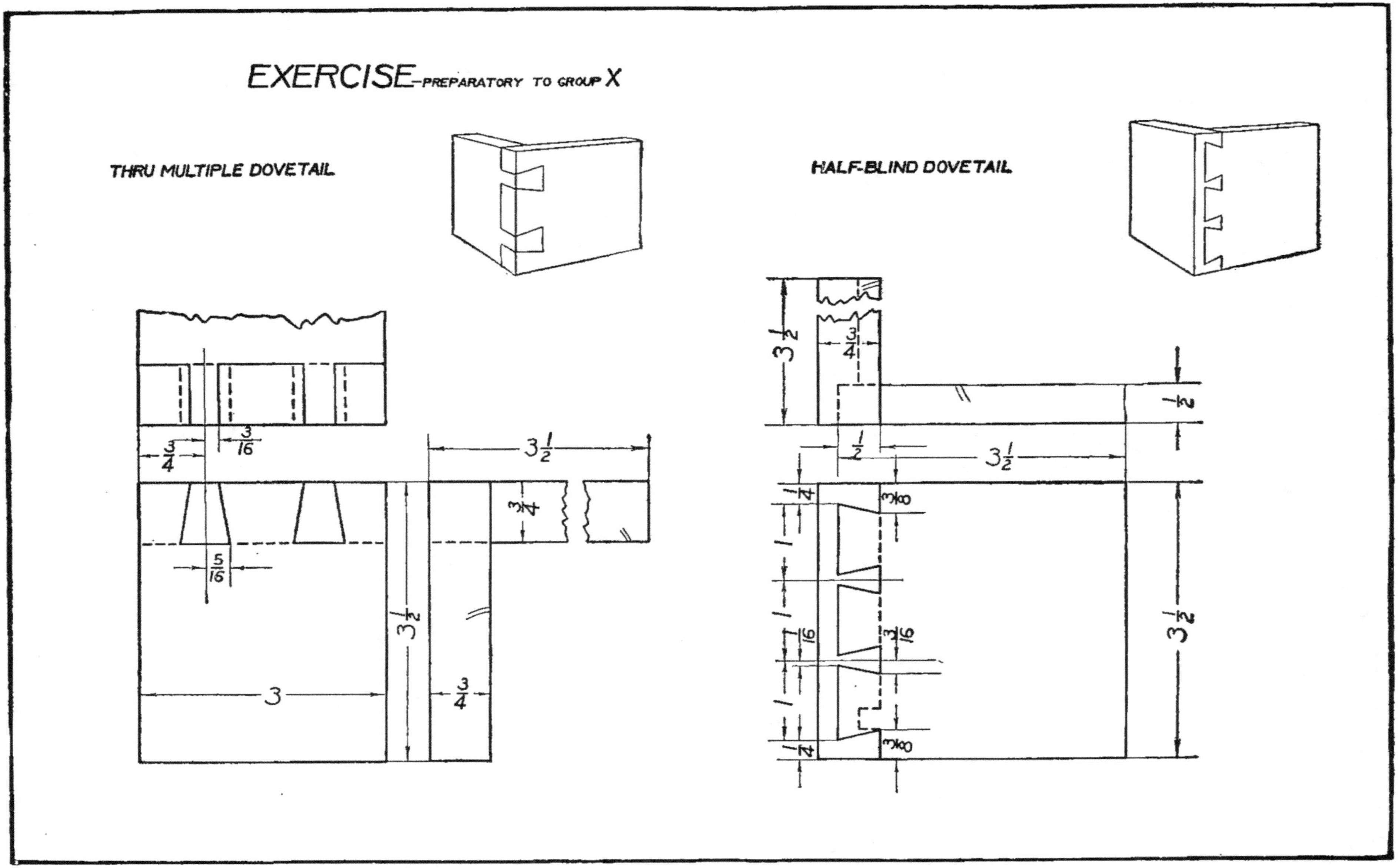

EXERCISE—PREPARATORY TO GROUP X
THRU MULTIPLE DOVETAIL
HALF-BLIND DOVETAIL
3/4
3/16
5/16
3 1/2
3
3/4
3 1/2
3/4
3 1/2
3/4
1/2
1/2
3 1/2
1/4
3/8
1
1
1/16
3/16
1
1/4
3/8
3 1/2

Plate 40

WASTE PAPER BOX

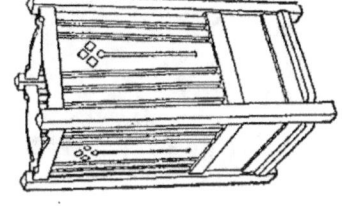
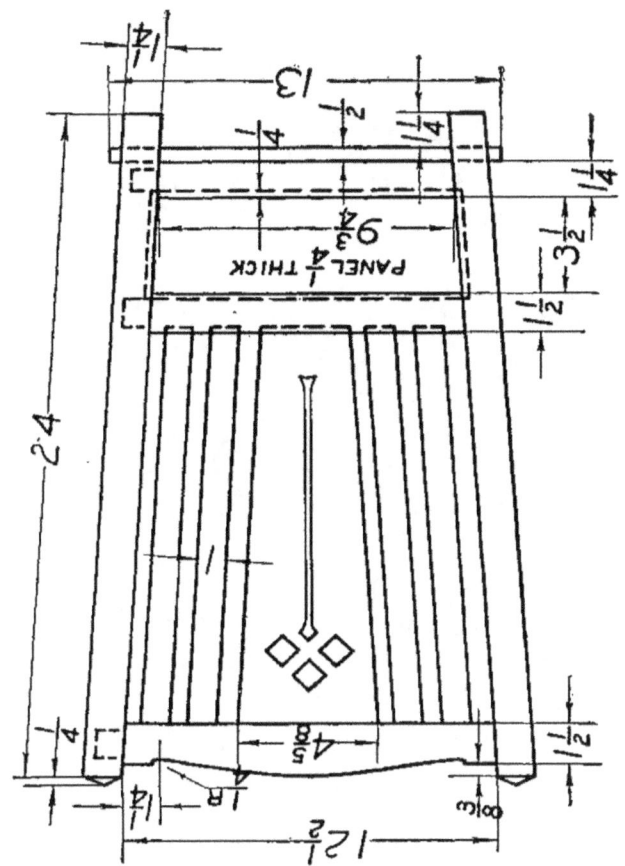
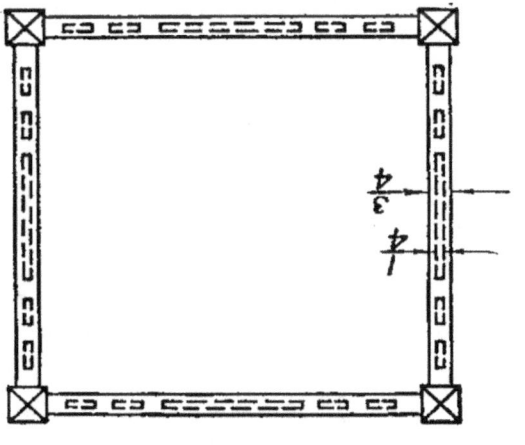

PLATE 41

WALL CABINET

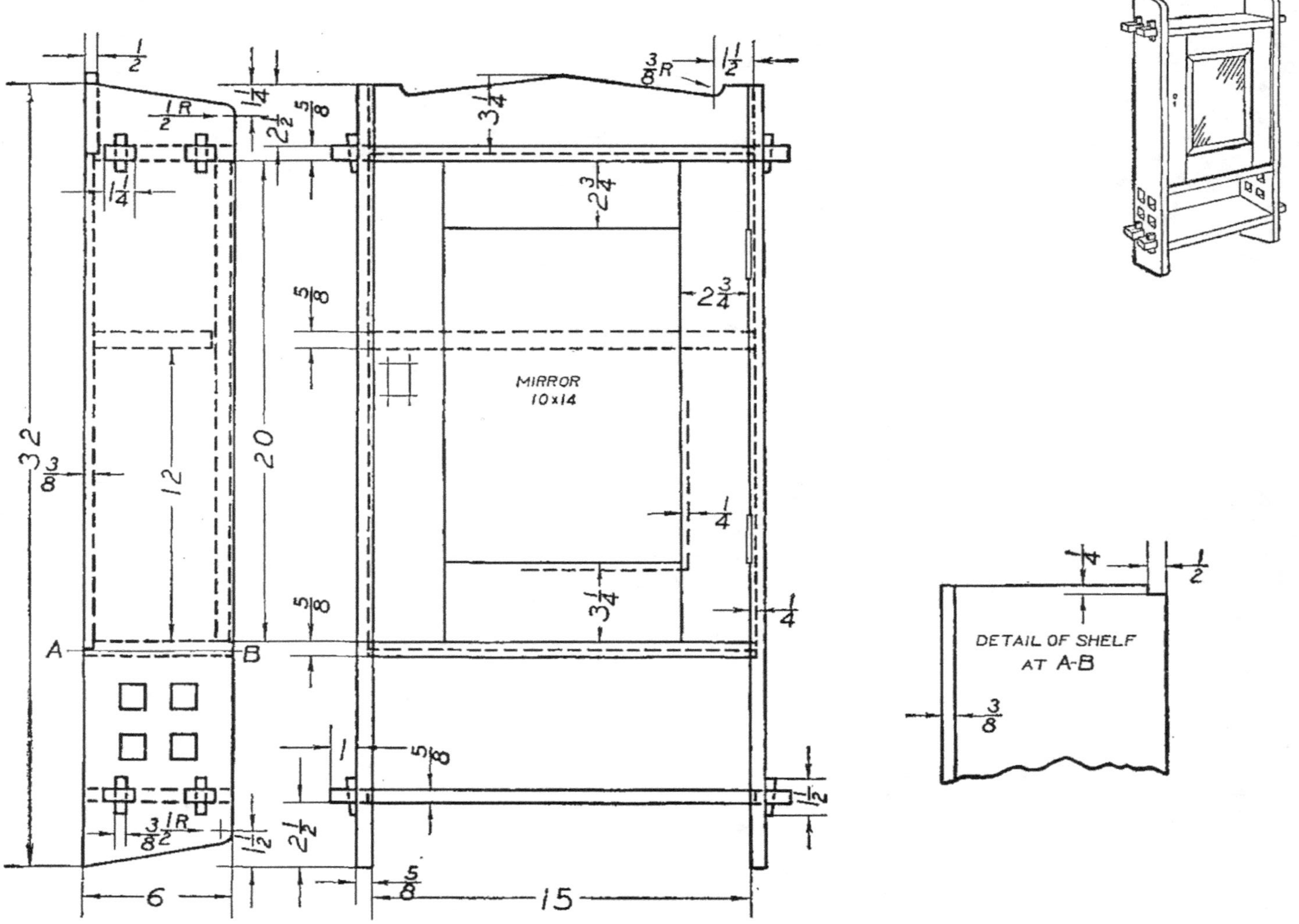

DETAIL OF SHELF AT A-B

MIRROR 10x14

PLATE 42

TELEPHONE TABLE

PLATE 43

SEWING CABINET

PLATE 44

WRITING TABLE

PLATE 45

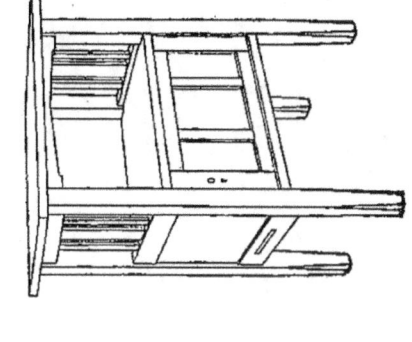
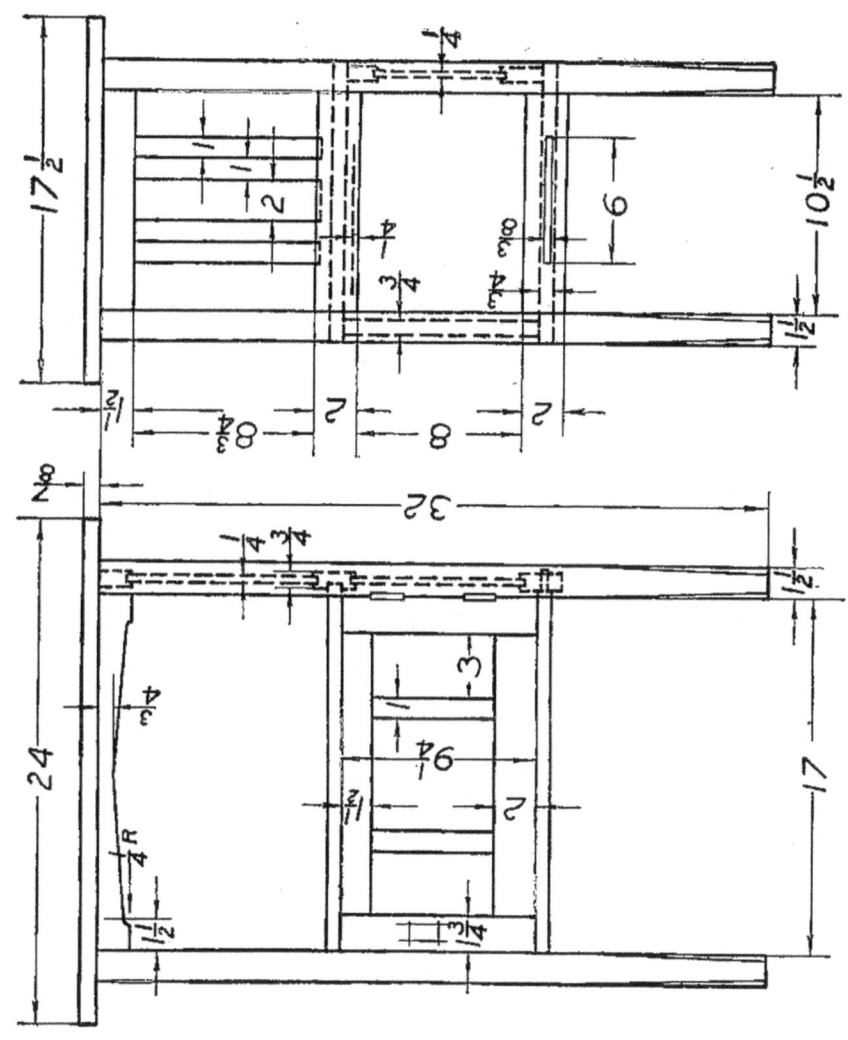

CHAFING DISH STAND

PLATE 46

CABINET

PLATE 47

LIBRARY TABLE

PLATE 48

WRITING DESK
7 1/2
1
3/4
12 3/4
1/2
12
5/8
3/4
41
8 1/2
3/4
1 3/4
14 3/4
16
4
5 1/4
1/4
3 1/2
23
3 3/4
30
10
3/4
26
COMMERCIAL DESIGN.

PLATE 49

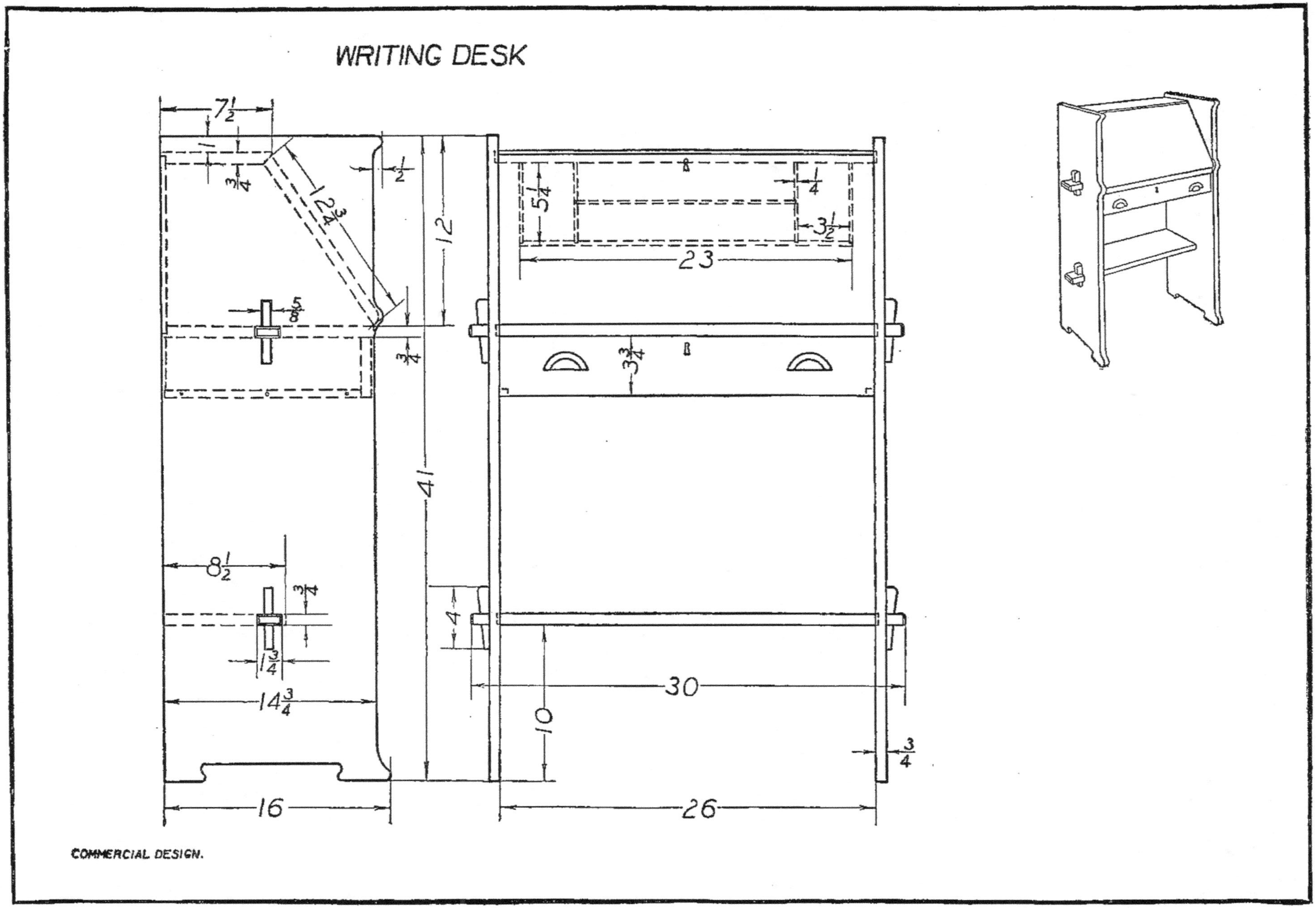

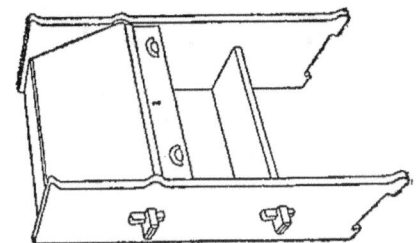

DRESSING TABLE

PLATE 50

LINEN CHEST
SECTION AT A-B
3/4
1/4
39
19 1/2
7/8
2 1/2
3
1/4
2 1/4
A
B
20
7 1/2
3
2 1/4
2 1/4
3/4
2 1/4
2 1/4
32
2
2
14

Plate 51

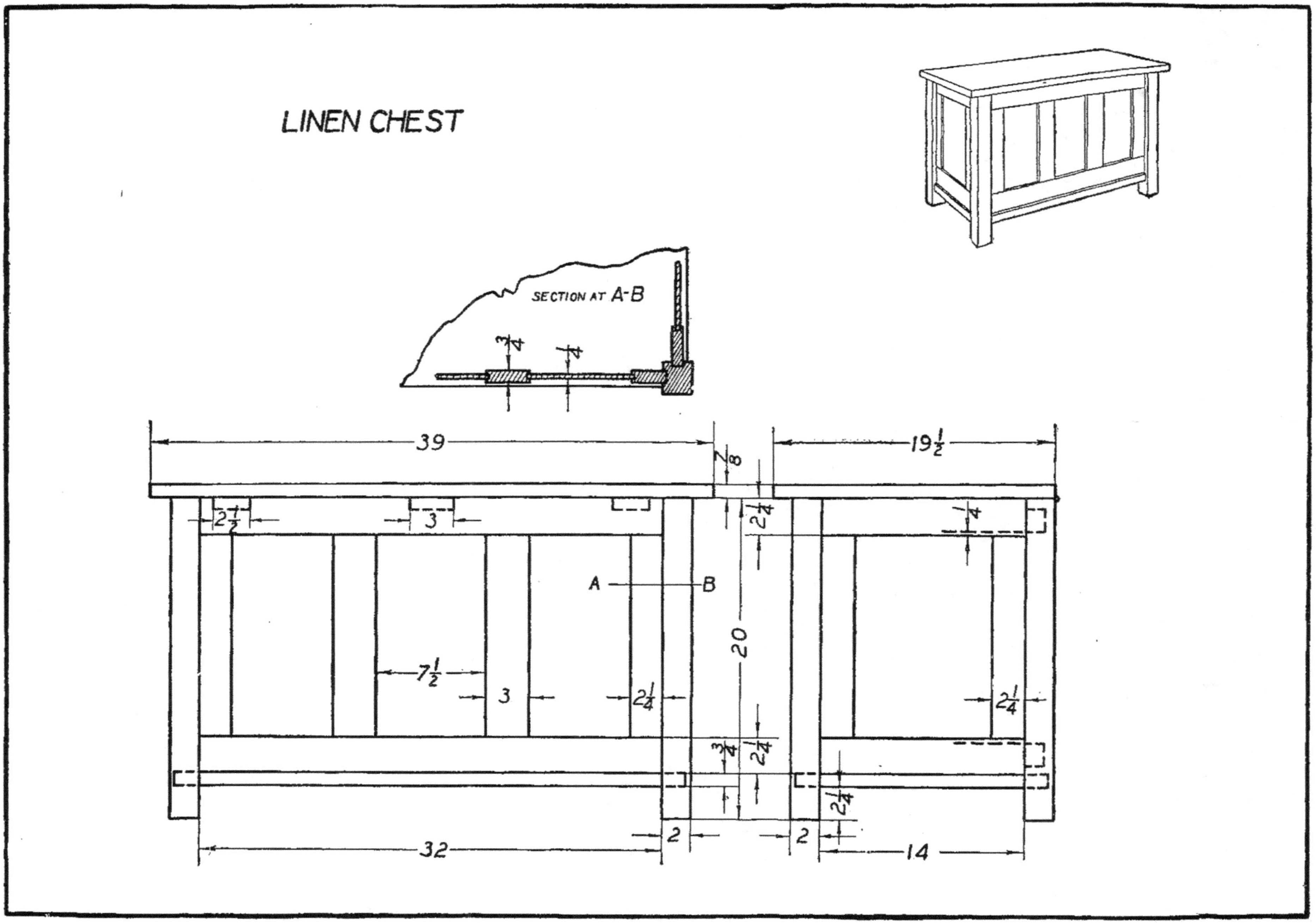

www.ingramcontent.com/pod-product-compliance
Lightning Source LLC
Chambersburg PA
CBHW051157290426
44109CB00022B/2497